I0132502

Simple Life

Poems

by

Richard Sievers

Simple Life
Poems

Copyright © 2013 Richard Sievers

All Rights Reserved

Field of Seven Houses Publishing
Battle Ground, Washington, USA
www.fieldofsevenhouses.com
www.fieldofsevenhouses@blogspot.com

ISBN:
Print Edition: **978-0-9829207-2-5**
Electronic Edition: 978-0-9829207-3-2

Library of Congress Control Number: **2012953112**

Cover Art and Design by Richard Sievers © 2013
Original Photograph by Richard Sievers: *Shannon in the Field* © 1972

For

Robbie
1956 - 1972

Our love never dies, brother.

Other Books by Richard Sievers

Morning Always Comes, Poems
© 2011
Field of Seven Houses Publishing

Earth My Body
© 2010
Field of Seven Houses Publishing

Books available
from the author (autographed copies): ricksfarm@yahoo.com
or amazon.com or lulu.com

Table of Elements

ABCDEFGHIJKLMNOPQRSTUVWXYZ
abcdefghijklmnopqrstuvwxyz
_-,!?.:;"~( )&@$/
0123456789

These are the
bricks and bombs
of thought and memory.
With these we create
whole worlds
or destroy a child.

This is the
miracle.
This is the
terror and wonder
of being human.

Table of Contents

Aging Again

Elements and Seasons

Wandering in Wonder

Ending

Dear Reader,

I am grateful for you.

I write this not only for my own expression and connection with my own life. I write this to reach across time and space, to make contact with you and to make the reading a healing experience. These words began as reflections of moments of this particular human being's life. I hope they grow and take on their own life. I hope they have bring you closer to the wild and precious life that is uniquely your own. Thank you for choosing this book.

Namaste'
Sanskrit for *I see you and I recognize the divinity within you.*
Rick
December 21, 2012

Prologue

Don't imagine your life more than you need to.

Practice of Spirit

Poem #1

Nothing here lives forever
unless the words slip
through the page
and into your chest.

Writing to Myself Writing to You

"Your work is to discover your work,
then, with all your heart, to give yourself to it."
Buddha

There is no time to lose.
Be true to your own
particular sensitivities.
You are not alone.
Make what is
universally private,
intimately public.

Daily Practice

A daily practice of disappearing:

So many ways to do this.

One is to be still.

One is to fly away.

Manly Development

I cried
reading a poem.
That is a good sign
for my development,
both the reading and
the tears.

Momentous

Novas of silence
orbiting a great song.
That's what I have:
intervals of eternity,
sun spun and shining
in a circle that once
appeared to be
a straight line.

Patience

I will hold
these words
close and wait:

      Do not flood
      love in a rush of fire.
      Let it bloom
      in its time,
      a late winter flower
      beside the stone, warmed
      in the low flung sunlight.

Raisin Bran

I don't want
to start the day
just thinking.
A bowl
of shimmering dreams,
a round garden
of fiery dew,
a golden globe
of sunflowers
lie before me
shining.

Two AM: Terrible Beauty

Orion rises in the east and
spins above my dreams.
Oh, what terrible beauty,
the consolation of being awake.

Four AM: Awake in the Dark

Restless.
Awakened.
Why?
Is it because I hear
the dreaming of ghosts?
Is it because I won't
believe the visions?
Or is it because I need
to see the truth
breathing in the dark?

On the Edge of Forever

I am circling around
the edge of sorrow.
I am a breathing dream.
I feel nothing.
Or do I feel everything?
All and nothing.
Is that what I feel?
Is that what I am?

Prayer While Traveling

I pray
>   so you will not be alone in your pain.

I pray
>   so I am not alone in my pain.

I pray
>   because my heart is bleeding with joy.

I pray
>   because the windows are rolled down
>   and I am driving into the sun.

Child's Pose

I love the way the pen glides and arcs across the page.
I wonder what it's like to die.
Will these words come with me?

Asana
Why Do I Cry in Yoga Class?

One day you're walking
along in sorrow and suddenly
it's all light. And the clouds
of broken stories are just
windows to fly through.

Nonsense

Trying
to
make
order
out
of
the
heart?
Go
ahead:
strip,
dissect,
scrutinize,
analyze,
penalize,
realize.

The
truth
makes
sense
only
to
the
soul
of
a
crazy
person.

How
can
we
argue
with
the
way
it
is
?

Loving and Being Loved

Your Storm

We met in the thunder.
Our daughter, we made in thunder.
Today, thunder fills the sky and shakes my body.
Your storm is my home.

My True Love

I felt your sweet kisses
fall upon me last night.
Heart to heart.
Flesh to flesh.
Dream to dream.
You breathed your true
yearnings into my ear.
And I answered
 "Yes. Yes."

Prophecy

In our long-ago dream
we kissed the stars
into each other's eyes.
Tonight, the memory of you
embraces me.
Mother, daughter, poet,
recall our sacred marriage
on the street corner?
My wild dark girl
dancing on the pavement,
where are the stars now?
"Make me you,"
you once whispered
to my spirit.
Then we came home
to the future of words
I still cannot speak.

What Her Ghost Said

It is better to love
the living
than the dead.

I'm alive.

Pineapple Express

A storm surge of tropical moisture in winter.

The storm is headed right
for us. A river of tropical memories,
a surge of the sun's heavy lifting,
the reminders to breathe between
the long and tangled sheets of history.

Every Poem

Every poem
I read,
I think
about you,
resting with
you between
the words.
Our joy
and sorrow
hovering just
above the page.

Fairy Breeze

In dreams I know
the touch of silken smiles
and fingers of ocean
dew upon my face.
When I awaken,
the moon has tumbled
into the green sea of grass.
The golden locks of sun
have fallen upon
the velvet shadows,
leaving a faint whisper,
a fairy breeze
dancing upon my lips.

Struggle to Evolve

At Day's End

I began the day with a song.
I finished the day in verse.
I thought it was a day like others.
I found bookends of divinity,
with sad little tales bound in between.

Writing in My Journal at a Little Wobbling Table in the Corner of the Coffee Shop While Feeling Small, Alone and Abandoned.

Witty winder of lost thoughts,
alone in the corner of the chatter,
sipping his essence
away with spoilt ink.
Are you tired?
Are you ready to be free?

The Dog Next Door Barked Again and Again

Dog barked all day.
Then he barked all night.
Boring when you analyze it.
Sad when you feel it.
Background noise when you set it down.
Like a thought or a compulsion.

Just under the Boil

Tea pot moans
just under the boil.
Rain has restrained herself
but threatens to
exhale at any moment.
Heart is trembling,
fluttering in the echo
of a dream it is
trying to recall.

Personality Trait That Led Me to Burnout

I am an unflappable chicken.

Wishing Myself out of Life

It'll be better on our island.
Over there,
across the strait.
Tourists would long to be
where I'd live with you,
over there,
in the grassy dew-dropped fields,
in a little house,
with you asleep,
over there.
We would be
happy, someday,
over there.

But the Weather Report Said:
Dry and Clearing

Water etches the window,
fills the field with tears,
floods the downspout
with a tinkling melody,
inundates my eyes
with sleepy wondering.

Who am I
if not a song
of a hidden star,
a particle of God,
an eye of the rain?

Planning to Live a Full and Happy Life
Someday Soon.
Really, I'll Get to It.
Almost Ready.
Just One More Thing.

Ok.
Almost
ready.
Plan
Plan
Plan

Ok.
Almost
ready.
Wish
Wish
Wish

Ok.
Almost
ready.
Die
Die
Die

RIP

Soul Reflected in the Mirror

My life is not
my own.
I am the god
you cannot see
until you are still,
looking into the gaze
of another being,
with heaven in one eye,
hell in the other.
The heart of
everything between
the two.

Prodigal

Now the long-lost
family has returned
the phone call.
At last.
Twenty dark years
of banishment remain
wedged in the dark
of the body,
while the eyes see
new light.

Storm, in Our Broken Trailer

The wind presses her black
face into the window pane.
Rain slants and moans
through frozen branches.
The writhing forest braces and
then surrenders to the storm.
Vishnu in the wind waves,
giver, receiver of our life together,
bends and breaks the world
into shiny little pieces.

Aging Again

Even the Gods Weep

Patient descent into myself,
with the grasses waving above my chest.
My hands held by the great ones
who have fallen and risen.
Then, like me,
they will fall again.
Even the gods weep.
So, I hold them
tenderly as I sleep.
Knowing their pains
of failure.
When I wake up,
I sing to them
from the hollow cradle
of my bones.

Old

A lot of living this week,
and tired, like a sack of old clothes
left in the roadside rain.

Methuselah

I am only
a shadow
in my own
body now.

I have longed
to reverse
this fade
into light.

And yet…
it is natural
to rise through
this bone cage,
moving out into
everything,
aware
that the flesh is both
freedom and
dungeon.

Epitaph in the Garden

I have a beautiful dream
rising from within the darkest part of me.
I feel its gentle hand, warm upon my shoulder.
My world is safe at last.
The garden has overwhelmed the drought.
The sun shines but never burns.

Death

There you are again,
dark lover.
Not yet; wait!
We have plenty of space
outside of time.
Please,
be still,
companion.
I have other friends
I still need to see.
But please tag along.
Your presence makes
this life sweeter
as my body sinks
closer and closer
to the mother of us all.

Grey Clouds Burning My Temples

I feel my life
turn.
Grey clouds are
boiling
as the intensity of
eternity
burns off the
tears of the past.

Arriving

After forty years of being a man,
I am not arriving anywhere
but here, in my heart.

Elements and Seasons

Coming Home in the Rain

Rain,
and I sit
at the writing
desk for the first time
since summer broke open
the blind bold face of the sun.

Air

There is no altar.
You are the altar.
Inspiration and expiration.
We only hold you
for a moment.
Then we give you away.

Why does the yogi
venerate the breath?
Why does the Shaman
fly on wings of sound?
Why does the Holy Spirit
arrive in the winds?
Why is the sky blue
when the air is clear?

The White Fire Rolled

The white fire rolled
and the Milky Way wept.
The snow began
a night of silences.
The hearth was banked with care.
The raven slept with the owl
behind the new moon.
Then, the morning sun danced
up from its dream of singing.

The round hearth smolders.
The earth stays hot
deep in her body.
Morning comes.
The fire remains.

The End of Summer

Harvesting and tilling.
Planting fall crops.
Making a new book
of old poems.

My decisions now
inform my future karma
of what is to be.

What do I wish to increase?
What no longer serves?

This moment creates
the future self or
tears it down.

The Molten Core

It's four thousand miles
to the earth's fiery center.
Solidity is not
as it appears on the surface.
There's mostly spaciousness
between the strings of atoms.
Far more energy than substance.
There really is nothing
between me and
the center of everything.

Spring

Will spring ever come?
The clouds wrap around
my head as a tourniquet.
And the storm in my eyes
coats all I see with sleet.
The sun pours out,
but no light comes in.
How long?
How long?
Will spring ever come?

Singing Today

The harvest has come in.
Clouds and compost are
heaped at the edge
of the field.
The sky lowers herself
in a curtsy, and cries
softly on the garden.

Wandering in Wonder

Fishing as a Boy

Trout:
I wonder how
you slipped away,
with your silvery shimmer
of thoughtless joy. You wandered past
the shining days of June, beyond the reach
of sun and storm. The crystal clear river taking your
wonder deeper into the swirling currents of my veins.

Shoreline

I've always been here.

When I die, the silence will fall like mist,
reflecting the sun, flickering and then fading,
being only a rippled coin toss on the tides.

I'll move in widening circles.

I've always been the water song,
shimmering and then still.

Did You See?

Did you see
the crescent moon,
her dark face held in
the silver cup?

I am free!

Did you see
how small I am,
so fragile,
so enraptured
by the moon?

So Many Ways
Mayne Island, BC

So many wines
to choose and
dive into:

> The waves and the brine,
> fluttering sky of stars,
> twilight raven songs,
> cabernet discussions,
> a woman's hand trembling.

So many ways to love the world.
So many ways to die.
So many ways to breathe.

Ending

Last Words

Let my last words be praises for Creation.
May my last thoughts be of The Beloved.
Praises for love.
Praises for our Creator, Healer and Lover.
Praises for Raven.
Praises for Her silk black nights and sunrises winging.

Praise our universe, you who continue on.
Praise the Creator, known and mysterious.
Praise the world, seen and unseen.

About the Author

Rick lives with his family on a small farm in Southwest Washington State, USA. In the Spring and Summer, he works with the soil and grows organic produce for his community and local farmer's markets. In the Fall and Winter he writes, trying his best to uncover the joy and sorrow hidden within words. He also spends time creating art from recycled objects, making sacred drums and facilitating writing circles.

Contact Rick at
ricksfarm@yahoo.com

Rick's Websites:
www.fieldofsevenhouses.blogspot.com
www.moonbearproduce.blogspot.com
www.fieldofsevenhouses.com

www.ingramcontent.com/pod-product-compliance
Lightning Source LLC
Chambersburg PA
CBHW031329040426

42443CB00005B/269